Nonsense Numbat

Pippa Bird

In the heart of the bush, where the sun shone bright,
Lived Larry the Lorikeet, who loved order and quiet.

One day he scolded,
with a voice rather loud,
his kids for their mess,
beneath a gum tree's
shroud.

"Chirp less, listen more,"
squawked the lorikeet with flair.
But his children just giggled,
tossing leaves in the air.

"Clean up this mess, you're
too wild," Larry cried.
His birdlings scrambled,
their joy pushed aside.

Perched on a stump, wise Nigel did see,
Larry's frustrations and lack of glee.

Nigel the Numbat,
with a heart true and kind,
decided to share
his wisdom in mind.

"Larry, my friend,
now listen, if you please.
Kids are naturally loud,
they buzz like the bees."

"To be messy and noisy
is just in their style,
It's part of their growing,
so let them be wild."

Larry then pondered,
his brow in a furrow,
"Chaos and noise,
how can I let go?"

"They're silly,"
smiled Nigel,
"And messy and loud.
But that's how
joy dances
in a gum blossom
cloud."

"The bush isn't quiet."
He said with a grin.
"Just listen to
kookaburras,
and feel wind
tickle your chin."

"The rustle of branches,
the wallaby thumps.
It's nature's own giggle,
in gum-nutty jumps."

"Embrace the nonsense,
embrace a loud, messy nest.
Where logic takes naps,
And laughter feels best."

Nonsense Numbat,
with a nod and a grin,
Said, "Embrace the commotion,
let the fun begin."

"To see their joy
and hear their
laughter all around,
will fill your heart's space
with a love so profound."

"Balance is key,
let them play, let them shout.
For this is what childhood
is truly about."

Larry looked at his kids,
playing with glee.
He let them be,
and flew up into the tree.

"Go on, have your fun!"
Larry called with delight,
"Just remember to tidy
when day turns to night."

The bushland was filled
with the sounds of pure cheer.
Messiness and noise
became welcomed and dear.

Larry the Lorikeet
learned from Nigel that day,
that joy comes from
letting kids be who they may.

More from this series by Pippa Bird

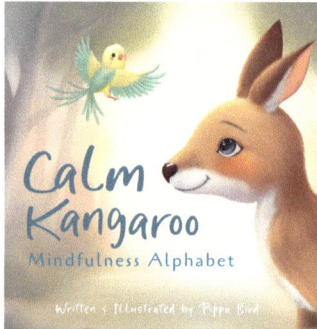
Calm Kangaroo — Mindfulness Alphabet
Written & Illustrated by Pippa Bird

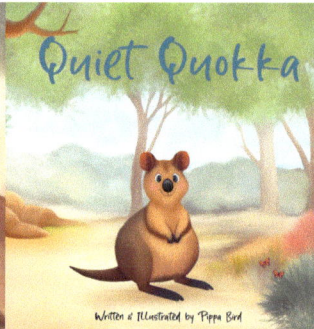
Quiet Quokka
Written & Illustrated by Pippa Bird

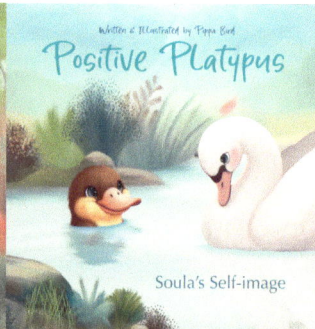
Written & Illustrated by Pippa Bird
Positive Platypus
Soula's Self-image

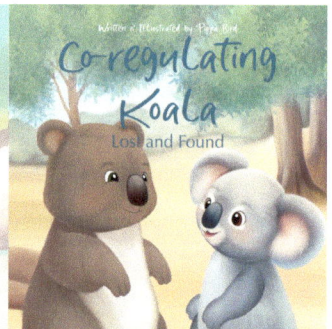
Written & Illustrated by Pippa Bird
Co-regulating Koala
Lost and Found

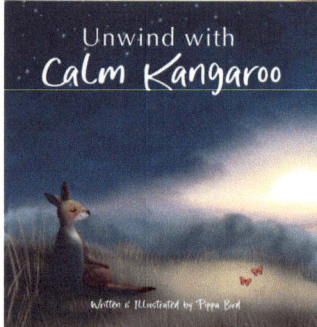
Unwind with Calm Kangaroo
Written & Illustrated by Pippa Bird

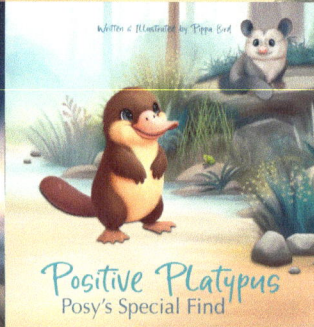
Written & Illustrated by Pippa Bird
Positive Platypus
Posy's Special Find

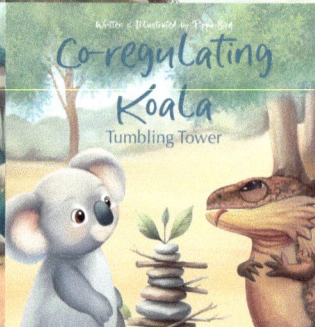
Written & Illustrated by Pippa Bird
Co-regulating Koala
Tumbling Tower

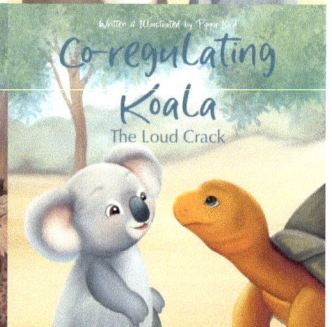
Written & Illustrated by Pippa Bird
Co-regulating Koala
The Loud Crack

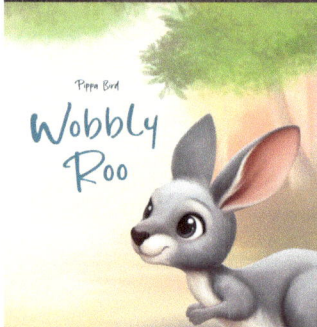
Pippa Bird
Wobbly Roo

Logical Lyrebird
Pippa Bird

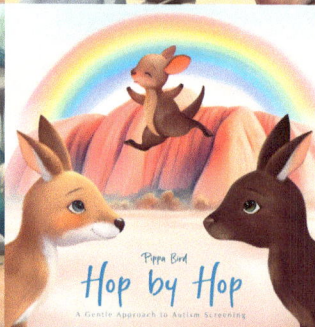
Pippa Bird
Hop by Hop
A Gentle Approach to Autism Screening

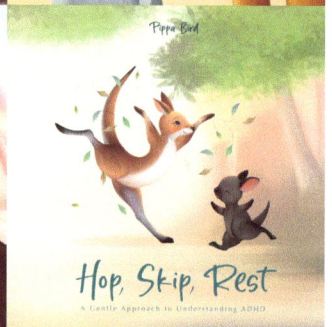
Pippa Bird
Hop, Skip, Rest
A Gentle Approach to Understanding ADHD

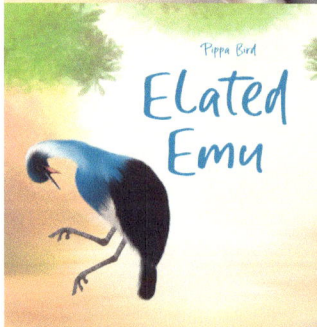
Pippa Bird
Elated Emu

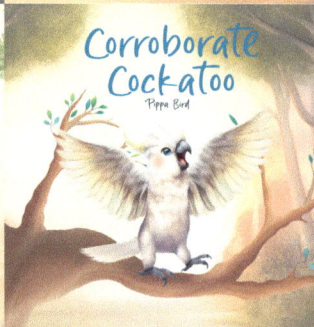
Corroborate Cockatoo
Pippa Bird

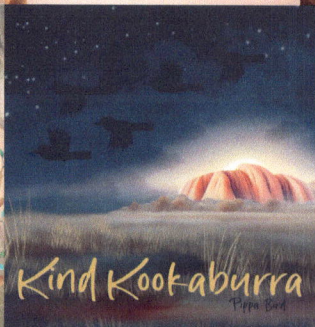
Kind Kookaburra
Pippa Bird

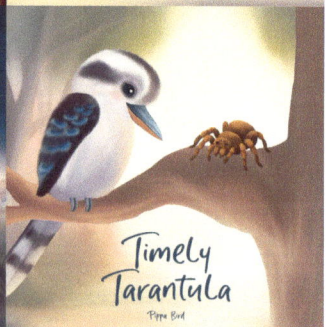
Timely Tarantula
Pippa Bird

www.ingramcontent.com/pod-product-compliance
Lightning Source LLC
LaVergne TN
LVHW072112070426

835509LV00003B/131

9 781763 833852